PERSISTENT

HOW TO FIND SUCCESS AFTER A TRAGIC EVENT IN **YOUR** LIFE

LUIS A ANDINO

Dedication

The book is dedicated to all the young
people struggling with life and all of those
parents and friends fighting to encourage
loved ones to find a reason to love who
they are and how valuable they are.

Special dedication to two friends we lost recently:

Carolyn Candelier-Jacome – She was part of a
very special group I mention in this book. Carolyn
was Persistent in her battle against a heart illness
while she also took care of her two sons. She was
a mother, a daughter, a sister and a friend.

William Martinez (Pupi) – He would make
you smile just looking at his sincere and lovely
attitude. Pupi was Persistent in finding ways
to bring joy to his family and friends with his
singing and contagious positive attitude. He
was a son, a brother and a friend.

Table of Contents

Introduction

Do you feel defeated? Do you have no desire or motivation to continue in the game of life?

I present to you the story of a teenager who went from a dependency on anti-depressants to finding success in every aspect of his life in less than 6 months.

This book is about perseverance and showing the world anything is possible. YOU CAN accomplish anything, no matter the situation.

I will be challenging you and the way you think.

There will be actions required to find the success you or your loved ones are looking for.

I can assure you, the lessons I learned and am sharing with you in this book absolutely work!

If you commit to read this book and really take ACTION, you WILL find the success you are looking for!

Follow the directions and lead your Life to a new Purpose. TAKE CONTROL TODAY!

CHAPTER 1

A Teenagers Life

I want you to think about one of the best times of your teenage years.

What did you do to make it the best? Who was part of your life to help you enjoy it? What was your routine?

One of the biggest components in a teen's life is to feel accepted by others—to "fit in."

The definition of "fit in" includes being part of a special group, or doing something everyone is doing to measure up to expectations.

Think about your own life and ask yourself: have you caved in to pressure to do something unwanted or unpleasant because you wanted to "fit in?" Did you hang out with the wrong crowd or take part in the wrong activities for popularity?

Perhaps you were even compelled to rush into love and get a boyfriend or girlfriend before you were ready. I believe an unspoken rule a majority of teens feel they need to adhere to is that you have to be with someone and go through what we will call love by a certain age.

I am the youngest of three brothers and I remember them constantly bringing girls over my house. The girlfriends hung out with us for long periods of time; I'm still not sure if my family was that good at entertaining or if they were just looking to escape their homes.

I felt very anxious around girls at school, especially on the first day of school, Valentine's Day, and Christmas time. I wanted to enjoy those special moments with a special person.

I would sometimes do things that didn't make sense just to make a girl I liked smile. For example I would shout something out in the middle of class to get that girl laughing, or skip class because the girl I liked was in recess.

A teenager doesn't just deal with the troubles of school, like assignments and homework. There is way more than that.

First of all, teenagers have to worry about bullies, and those bullies are often your so-called "friends." They are the ones that take advantage of you because you studied and did your homework, so they try to copy you. This kind of bully is even more dangerous because there is a belief that if you don't do what they ask, you are not being a true friend.

Teenagers also have to deal with teachers that just don't like you every single day. Some teachers even say things like, "You are not going to make it," or "You will be nothing in life," or even "Just give up. You will not pass my class."

The worst thing I believe teenagers have to deal with is the situation of "liking" someone for the first time and experiencing something you have never experienced before. This makes you feel like you are not in control of your own mind, causing distractions and keeping you from succeeding in other areas. When you are in this state, some days they feel like Christmas because you are excited to even see from a distance that special individual. Other days, you don't even want to go to school because of something that happened with this individual. Sometimes you don't even know how to feel about certain awkward situations with this individual.

Fast forward to the year 2000 . . . Y2K and so many other legends people said, like the end of times and judgement day and many, many other crazy things . . .

Everything was fine and the future was as bright as it could be.

I graduated high school in 1999 and was going to a college next to my main job not far from home. I had some friends from school joining the same college as well.

5

PERSISTENT

I had 3 jobs at the time: my main job was in the mall working in a clothing store, my second was in college working in the bookstore, and my third job was with my mom, making and selling bakery items out of our home.

Everything was going well at home. I recently got a new car and invested some money in making it look good inside and out.

I had been dating a girl for about 3 years and in my mind we were practically "married" already. We did everything together. We were in the same college and I helped her find a job next to mine. Her family was one of the most united families I had ever seen and I enjoyed spending time with all of the many aunts and cousins.

Not too long after, in October, 2000, I got recruited to work in a new company selling electronics. This was a month that changed my life forever!

Do you remember a particular time in your life where things took a turn? Do you regret what happened? Do you believe it was part of the plan? Maybe this is something happening right now.

We should always welcome change, because it comes with new opportunities and horizons to reach.

I believe no matter what situation a teenager is in, it is up to those around them (parents, uncles, aunts, grandmas, grandpas, neighbors, teachers, coworkers and everyone else in their life) to help them make good decisions.

When adults take responsibility to make our homes a better place and focus on the teenagers which are the future of our society, there is a better chance of making the world better for tomorrow's generations.

Let's take a look at what teenagers are saying, according to stageoflife.com, a website about age groups:

- 76% of teens would rather check out nature outside on a hike than check out friends' statuses on Facebook.

- 34% of teens like the music their parents listen to.

- 86% say they enjoy school.

- 57% of students play sports outdoors with their family.

- 77% of teens say they have read at least one extra book for personal pleasure.

- 73% feel their appearance affects their body image.

- 51% of teens are afraid of talking to their parents about personal problems.

- 83.5% of teens pay attention to the news.

- 90% of students spend more time with their family in the summer.

- 90% of teens love their country.

- 42% of students say they experienced their "moments of awesomeness" with their friends and 27% say they have with family.

- 1 out of 4 says it's easier to remember the negative/bad moments in their life than good moments.

- 75% of students set goals for themselves.

- 97% of students learned their manners from home.

- 73% of high school and college students know someone who is taking medication because of a mental health issue.

- 1 out of 2 teens state they have struggled with mental illness at some point.

- Depression and anxiety ranked #1 & #2 as the most suffered mental illness by teens.

- 61% of teens have been "in love."

- 94% of teens believe in true love.

- 92% of teens want to get married at some point in their lives.

- 60% of high school students plan to break-up with their current girl/boyfriend when they leave for college.

- 39% of teens have NOT told their parents about their current relationship.

I want you to keep in mind a teenager or someone in your life going through a tough time and how you may be able to help them. Maybe this person is you.

Chapter 1 Notes

Chapter 1 Notes

Chapter 1 Notes

CHAPTER 2

The Call

Have you ever received a call that disturbed your sleep? Usually a call coming very early in the morning or late at night is NOT a good call. Those calls usually start with, "Are you Mr./Mrs. _____?" and continue to say, "My name is Officer_____," or, "I'm calling from _____ Hospital."

The night of November 4th 2,000, I had gone to bed early and was sleeping when the call came through at around 9:00 p.m. I recognized the number as my girlfriend's number, but there was a very unfamiliar voice on the other side. A male voice, I was worrying to death that she may be in harm's way. The words coming out of this individual had a threatening message for me specifically. He expresses the fact he was from a bad neighborhood known for their criminal activity.

My adrenaline, concern, and anger were overwhelming. There was no time to get properly dressed. I left in flip flops. I had suspicions of where she was last, and I was able to confirm it with some calls I made to friends & family members while I was driving.

She was in my neighborhood.

Something was very distressing and not right. Once again the thoughts of anger, confusion, and distress overpowered my common sense and my ability to think. All I remember seeing were the doors of a car closing rapidly as I approached a playground area with no streetlights. I'd never seen this vehicle and I didn't have any idea who was in it . . . I just had a gut-wrenching feeling she was inside.

My mom and other neighbors remember that night and the noise my car and theirs made as I chased them through the streets (15-miles speed limit) at over 60 miles-per-hour. I can't tell you how many times we came close to crashing, or how many times I felt like I was losing control of the vehicle as it moved recklessly. My mind kept repeating again and again, *she's in trouble and you need to get her out of there!* It felt like a long time, but it was just seconds before we got out of the housing area. I chased them down a long road that takes visitors and residents out of the housing community. I tested the miles-per-hour indicator that day as I pushed my car to over 120 miles. The indicator was all the way to the end, bending the needle. This was a good illustration of my feelings that night . . . I was ready to surpass the limits and go all the way until I could get her out of harm's way.

THE CALL

This was not a race, make no mistake about it, this was about getting this car to stop. I didn't have any idea what to do after I got the car to stop. I didn't know what to say to the driver or how to help her to get out of the car safely . . . but I chased them anyway. I had no choice.

A curve came, and with it a loud noise and partial unconsciousness. The two cars crashed together, and I spiraled until the car crashed into a cement light post, almost breaking the car in half.

There was a ringing in my ear as I started to gain consciousness, then all the noises came in at once: tires running, broken glass crushing as I make my first moves, the door dangling on its hinge, and in the distance, the street.

Fueled by adrenaline, I struggled to open the mangled door. As I got out of the car I realized I was in the middle of cows and horses corral. I saw some people in the distance, but the blood in my eyes didn't help me to make up a clear vision of them.

The walk to the street was heavy like I was carrying weights in my feet . . . every step felt heavier and heavier until I touched the pavement and immediately felt disturbing pain!

Barbed wire! The corrals always have barbed wire to keep the animals for leaving or people from the outside entering.

It felt very much like a slow motion scene from a horror movie as I looked down and I see my feet, protected only by flimsy flip flops, bloody and wrapped in barbed wire. I screamed, inside out with painful agony and desperation. I was dragging this wire with my feet for about 100 meters until I came to the street.

Getting closer to the 3 individuals and now able to see more clearly, I came into the realization very quickly that my girlfriend was never in real danger. My girlfriend was attending to this individual I didn't know with concern and was trying to give consolation. At that moment my mind had many questions, and my body wanted to react.

I don't remember anything about the third person, and to this day I don't care. The only thing I cared about was seeing my girlfriend of over three years destroy our relationship involving both our families and hundreds of very special times together in one night. It was clear to me that she was cheating and had an ongoing romantic relationship with this guy.

The tables turned very quickly as everyone started pointing at me. Angry words came out their mouths on this cold night on a tropical island, close to an area where the beach breeze can be seen and felt distinctively.

What? Wait . . . I was NOT the bad guy!

How can I be the bad guy if I was in my bed sleeping in my home with no issues and *they* made a call to *my* phone and disturbed my peace? Regardless, they certainly were treating me like the bad guy.

In my life I have come to the realization that the key to avoiding confrontation and being the better person is to be humble and move on. We have too many tragedies happening because of pride:

- Neighbors hurting each other—sometimes with words and sometimes physically.

- Brothers fighting with each other.

- Best friends not talking anymore.

- Families disintegrating.

- Pride could take us to the worst outcome: a decision of deadly consequences.

I asked myself for years after this event why I got out of bed that night. Was it pure concern for my girlfriend, or was it the idea of not being in control?

Take a moment to ask this question yourself. Do you remember a time where the real reason you were mad had more to do with pride than any other feeling?

It is amazing and perplexing what a human being will do when they feel there is nothing they have control over.

This is one of the main issues we see today on our daily lives; this is a delicate situation that often ends in tragedy:

- The student trying to focus on school who also has to deal with bullies every single day . . . what control do you think they feel they have?

- How about the child in an abusive relationship with a close family or friend . . . what control does this child feel they have?

- The wife who feels guilty when the husband tells her she is nothing and puts his hands on her. What control does she have?

In every one of those, we see endings with someone getting marked for life—or in some cases, we see someone taking a life!

Coming back to the accident where I was identified as the bad guy, I realized my life almost ended.We were in the middle of the street and there was no sign of any cars passing by. The closest area to ask for help was at least 45 minutes away on foot, and I didn't know where my phone was to be able to make a call.

Now, let's look at this moment from the advantage point of my mother, who only heard cars driving fast and knew I was not home.

Our actions have consequences, especially for the people who care very much about us and our well being.

Take a moment now and remember those who love and care about you. If you are in a difficult situation, they will hurt and suffer with you (I encourage you to call them to thank them for caring about you and your well being).

We all have at least one person that cares for us and will do anything to get us out of harm's way . . . she sacrificed herself for nine months to give us life and sustained our fragile body when in her womb.

She has been there for you when you had your struggles as an infant, toddler, child, teenager and now adult . . . treasure your mother very much every day. Some of you may have a special guardian like a grandmother or even an uncle or another special person that took the role of parent in your life. That special person will suffer your lost battles and will also rejoice in your WINS!

My mom was not with me and at this moment when I knew there was nothing I could do to control the situation. I had one of those moments we all have, when we say, "I need my mom."

There was a chatter going around between the other three. I knew there was anger, confusion, sadness, and some type of regret for all four of us, and we were all probably asking the same questions: how did we come to this moment? What do I do to fix it? What's next?

Chapter 2 Notes

Chapter 2 Notes

CHAPTER 3

The Aftermath

The tire marks were fresh in the pavement and the smell of burned break liquid was fresh in the air. Four people were in the middle of the street with no cars passing by.

Take this time to remember the most intense situation you have been part of . . . what was it? What did you see as the possible outcomes? Which outcome did you choose, and did you choose wisely?

I could run, I could start a fight, or I could just wait and see if someone passes by to take a ride with them.

After all these thoughts, someone did show up and I do think, looking back, this was a sign someone was looking after me from above.

I got in the car and it was actually someone that I knew from my neighborhood. They asked questions about the accident and they called 911.

The ride was less than ten minutes long, and there were a lot of thoughts coming through my mind. I introduced myself to the option of taking my own life. I don't have a car, I don't have my girl that I care so much about, and on top of it all I also didn't have my dignity because of how I handled the situation. I felt I was a coward the way I dealt with it. I found my girlfriend was cheating and I didn't stand tall to confront the situation. I found out she was not in danger and I didn't react like I should have. I saw the guy who had disturbed my peaceful sleep and I should have punched him in the face or hit him with a rock . . . something other than doing nothing.

They took me home. My mom reacted the most motherly way she could have, asking, "What happened to you? Where were you?"

She saw a bloody body with head, feet, leg, and arm injuries. Somehow I was "okay." I didn't feel any-thing was broken and I didn't feel the need to go to a hospital.

At this point my mom had already made calls to see if someone knew where I was and many people already knew I was missing. She called them all back and let them know she found me. My dad usually took over an hour to get from where he lived to us, but that time he got there in 30 minutes.

My mind was full of negative messages and I continued to hear a voice saying, "You don't have anything to live for anymore. Your family is suffering because of you. What are you going to do to end this?"

When my mom took me to the scene of the accident, the police and ambulance were getting there too. I remember the police saying something to my mom that can destroy a mother's life in seconds—that at only 19 years old I could be accused of attempted murder. Three witnesses said I crashed intentionally into their car. How does someone go from sleeping peacefully in their bed to being accused of attempted murder in a couple hours?

It was a moment of desperation. My life would be ruined forever and I may go to jail! What could I have done? I felt there was no way out of it except ending my nightmare of a life now!

I started to drift away from the area and got closer to the streets where cars were passing by. There were no lights in the street, and my plan was to lie down so the cars couldn't see me and take the hit. I was already weak from the accident so I figured it would be easy.

Do you know someone that may be starting to drift away? Maybe this is your situation. Do you feel you have the need to get this life over with? According to Stageoflife.com, the second leading cause of death in the 10-24-year-old group is suicide, and suicide attempts occur 20 times more frequently than complete suicide. Suicide rates have increased 60% worldwide in the last 45 years!

I don't remember who, but someone screamed. Next thing I knew someone pulled me out of the street just before a car was coming toward where I lay on the pavement.

Looking back, it is very surprising I didn't go to jail or a rehabilitation center after the different things I did and the testimony against me.

My mom did a great job of explaining to the officer the story of me and the other three individuals. Believe it or not, the fact I had flip flops on may have helped me stay out of jail that night. I did look like someone just woke up, and the other three didn't.

The decision seemed quick and everyone was in agreement. I will go with my dad and stay with him for a while. I left the scene to pick up some things at home. As Dad's car took me away, I felt hopeless. I even tried to open the door of the car at some point to jump out!

I don't remember any words that came out of my mouth or my dad's mouth. What does a dad have in his mind when he is dealing with this type of situation? Where can parents find the strength to confront a child's desire to die? What actions or steps could they take?

There are many resources now, but at that time I don't recall the topic of suicide at all like we see it today . . .

Nobody was able to sleep that night. My mom didn't, my dad didn't and I certainly didn't.

Saturday night was over, and Sunday started with a dark reality. I woke up knowing vividly that what happened yesterday wasn't a nightmare, but my new reality. I remember going to the restroom, looking in the mirror, and having the thought to end my life with pills. My dad already removed the pills the night before and I was not able to complete my thoughts with actions.

I couldn't help but wonder why I still had a life. What reason did I have to exist after all the events taking place? There were multiple times I should have died, and I couldn't understand how I was still here.

What do I still have? It was like a battle in my mind. Part of me wanted to move on and part of me was only interested in feeling like a failure.

What do we still have when tragedy comes through the door to knock us down?

I had a family that loved me very much, I had friends that cared very much about me and my wellbeing, and I had a new job that I started weeks before.

We have to find a reason to not give up. Our actions are determined by what we think and how long we keep those thoughts in our head.

Can we train our mind to be positive? And can we train our mind to be negative? Both answers are yes! But *how* can we train our mind to be positive after a tragedy?

I made a decision to win in my new job. Why not? I have it and I'm not about to lose that, too!

After the accident I went back to work and I found a new spark that ignited my desire to succeed and WIN!

What is the one thing you have in your life that keeps you going, sparks your mornings, and keeps you alert and ready to WIN every day?

Even though I started to find new ways to motivate myself, there is no question that mentally I suffered a great damage and it would take some time to heal.

Next I will address some of the issues someone goes through in a tragic event and how they get to a place of not appreciating life any more.

Chapter 3 Notes

Chapter 3 Notes

CHAPTER 4

Meaningless Life

Mental health is a hot topic these days. I don't know if we actually have a solution for this threat our society has to endure every single minute, hour, and day.

Why do we see people taking their life when everything looks good in the surface? Why is it that teenagers are doing unimaginable things, like harming themselves or others?

What is in their mind and what are their struggles?

Before we attempt to answer those questions, let's take a look at some of the most recognizable root cause of mental health issues or illness:

-Anger: a strong feeling of annoyance, displeasure, or hostility. Psychologytoday.com defines Anger as a corrosive emotion that can run off with a person's mental and physical health.

Is holding anger in the solution? Or is it better to let it all out?

PERSISTENT

Have you ever seen someone angry? Like, *really* angry? When someone is angry at someone else, it is a controllable situation. The two people decide the fate of the situation and how to handle it. On the other hand, when someone is angry at them and finds guilt for things they did or didn't do; it could be more difficult to deal with. Sometimes anger is deep inside, and you don't see it until an event causes the emotion to reveal itself.

We need to pay attention to our loved ones and make sure someone is not inhibiting anger for a long time. My recommendation is to take care of your issues today. Don't go to sleep angry, because you will probably have a much harder time fixing the issue later (if you get to it).

In my case, at first I felt angry at other people for disturbing my peace and putting me in this situation. Little by little I started feeling guilt for disturbing my mom's peace, for letting my feelings get in front of reason, for not having control of myself, and for just making bad decisions. The subject of my anger was shifting from others to me.

I called myself stupid, unworthy, ignorant, weak, coward, powerless, purposeless, lonely, loser, and many more. This is when I started to think there was no purpose of living if I was all those things.

This is when YOU, as a parent or friend can help. Even if you are mad at someone and you would like to say the infamous "I Told You So," DON'T do it!

Those who are suffering need you to be there with us and to tell us all the great decisions we made and how proud you are of us, despite our mistakes.

Please, please, understand this is not about someone going through a trauma. This is about someone going throughout life. The kid in school receiving C's and D's is already thinking, "I'm stupid, I'm a loser, I'm dumb" and more. He is coming home already dying inside because he knows the reaction his parents will have. When parents and friends start repeating the things he already has in his head, they are enabling the kid to confirm what he thought he already knew.

I've learned in my experience working with youth that we need to ask more questions, re-affirm the facts, and move into solutions. Challenge the kid, "There is nothing we can do about the past, so what are you going to do now? And how can I help?"

If you don't have any idea whether or not your kid is failing in school and you are taken by surprise by their grades, well . . . what does that say about your involvement with your children? What are you going to do to be more present next time?

I am a firm believer that the biggest issues we have in our country and the world right now is parents who are not caring about their kids' education. The teachers in my family tell me this all the time. Parents don't come to meetings and they don't get in touch with the teacher about their kids' progression. It's a very sad situation and we need to do something!

If you ARE this kind of parent, what are you going to do today to change this narrative? If you HAVE this kind of parent, what are you going to do to help them be more involved?

Write down at least 3 actions you will take today:

1–

2–

3–

Like anger, anxiety is a normal reaction to stress and can be beneficial in some situations. It can alert us to dangers and help us prepare and pay attention. Anxiety disorders, however, differ from normal feelings of nervousness or anxiousness and involve excessive fear. According to psychiatrist.org, anxiety disorders are the most common mental disorder, affecting 30 percent of adults at some point in their lives. But anxiety disorders are treatable, and treatment helps most people with anxiety live normal, productive life. Last year I was traveling by air at least once per week, and it was evident flying is one of the most anxious times for many people, especially those who are traveling for the first time.

We worry about things we can't control. This is one of the major issues about anxiety. My fearless leader Tim (executive in the company I work), who has inspired my life inside and out of work, always said . . . "You can't fight gravity. If you want to challenge gravity, well, you will probably lose." There is nothing you can do about an object dropping from above and hitting the ground. You could slow it down, but it will still hit the ground. That's gravity!

At the same time, we need to learn to control our emotions and thoughts when it comes to things we just can't control.

I couldn't control the decisions of other people in the traumatic situation I mentioned before. I could influence, but not controlled. Can you control the decisions a pilot makes in midair while a storm is coming? Not at all!

I was worried about families. I was worried about the time we spent together and how that was going to affect our mutual friends. I was worried about how I could fix this to help my loved ones not suffer because of my decisions.

A father seeing their kids are hungry will get anxiety, and will probably start doing simple things to take care of the issue. They believe is all in their control and maybe at some point if they can't find a job or get help the thought will be to steal from someone else. The father *believes* this is within his control and he SHOULD resolve this issue for his family as the provider!

What if the situation was different and the father has their son in jail? How will the father ensure their son will eat? Is he in control of this situation? No, things have gone into a different level. There is nothing they can do by themselves because they don't have control over anything that happens in those facilities. They will probably visit their son and see if he seems weak or if he lost weight. Maybe they will start asking questions to see if they need to influence something with the administration. They still take some kind of action and they can help impact the situation, even though they are not in control.

I couldn't control any of the things I was worried about. The only things I could control were my feelings and emotions, which were all in disarray.

Focus on what you can control, and you will be on your way to win the battle against anxiety.

Write down at least 3 actions you will take today, focusing in your circle of control:

1—

2—

3—

Depression is classified as a mood disorder. It may be described as feelings of sadness, loss, or anger that interfere with a person's everyday activities. According to MedlinePlus.Gov, 19 million teens and adults in the United States suffer from depression.

Depression is very scary, because while anger and anxiety are tough to deal with, they can be overcome by a simple treatment. Depression is the product of years of anger, anxiety, or both. There are treatments for depression which require multiple resources and consistency creating good habits. MedlinePlus.Gov recommends therapy and counseling, including brain situation therapies.

People get depressed over things they just can't deal with anymore. They may feel defeated, perhaps because of a goal or a plan not coming to fruition. Or maybe they lost someone they loved. Depression can occur due to a variety of circumstances that make one feel like "everything is lost".

Depression can cause other major issues like obesity, drug addiction, suicidal thoughts, and more dangerous situations for you and your loved ones.

I was very much defeated and depressed. I was thinking there was no other way to get out of this nightmare beyond ending my life. Some people eat lots of food when they are depressed, but I was completely the opposite. I was 19 years old at 5'10, yet at a low point I weighed 90 pounds. Let that sink in for a second.

I started taking antidepressants, but it was very scary how those pills changed the way I felt and thought. If a pill that changes you behaviorally doesn't scare you, I don't know what can!

Have you or someone you know reach a low point in their life?

Maybe the person you have in mind is closing their doors and living in a solitary world. Maybe this person doesn't value themselves and can't find a reason to be happy or even smile at all.

What I have found is that it doesn't matter what situation you or your loved ones are facing, there are always things you can look forward to. Chances are, you or those you love are going through something in their lives that is keeping them from appreciating their reasons to live. They have a lot more to fight for than they realize.

What if?

What if you shift your Anger to a new goal and a new purpose? What will be the results, and how will you change your mood and mindset?

There are many studies according to betterhelp.com about dropping all your anger in a ball park or coliseum. The reality is that you can shift your anger to a new project in the house, a pastime job at a demolition site, or taking it out on the punch bag at the gym. These practices become a very healthy way of dealing with anger & anxiety, and at the same time you are having lots of fun.

What if your anxiety became excitement? According to healthcentral.com, many studies have shown people often feel anxious when confronted with a specific task or something new they haven't experienced before. The studies focus on shifting mental thoughts from "I'm scared, I'm anxious" to "I'm excited." This simple exercise changes the way you feel, and your thoughts become more positive.

What if you battle depression with exercise?

I know, this one is well known and feels too difficult. There is no time, you don't want to go to a gym, I get it. But, it's true that one of the best ways to deal with depression is through exercise.

Start with one minute every day. Start with some type of action getting you closer to your goal. One minute today doing jumping jacks is more than o yesterday, correct? Start today!

Do you know someone that needs help starting an exercise routine? Help them get through step one: starting! One minute will become two, and four, eight and so on.

I challenge you to do something today and make yourself better tomorrow, whatever the situation.

PERSISTENT

Help someone else become better if you think you are good already.

Chapter 4 Notes

Chapter 4 Notes

CHAPTER 5

Solutions

I was about to embark on a journey with two distinct purposes: to reach my goals in my new job, and to find peace in all the negative life events affecting me and my loved ones.

At work, I was introduced to a new goal/milestone called Caribbean Jewel. I needed to reach a certain amount of sales with a combination of high productivity in one month. When I first had a conversation with my co-workers, they were very skeptical this could be done by a rookie. I was very persistent and I did my research. I was determined to meet this goal. On the other hand, I was also dealing with court hearings and therapy with many expert sources including a priest, natural medicine, and everything else I needed to do.

However, the suicidal thoughts didn't just go away. This is something really important for parents to understand. Just because someone is getting better and found a reason not to be dead, it doesn't mean they still don't think about it time to time. They may even start wondering what will happen if the thoughts stay until the mind is healed. The best way to deal with this is through staying physically and mentally busy so there is no time to daydream or have nightmares.

Many times we try to find the answer in professionals, even when we know our parents and loved ones know more about us than any other human being.

Think about someone you love and know very well. Do you know what they dream about? Do you know their goals? Do you know what makes them happy as a kid on Christmas morning?

I challenge you to come up with the answers to the questions above.

Take 10 minutes and write your loved one's name and the answers down below:

1—

2—

3—

If you are having trouble with these answers, then answer this: what can you do to know your loved ones better?

SOLUTIONS

Do you understand what I'm trying to say here?

Think about a friend that you know is having a rough time. If you knew this friend loves to go to the park and picnic would you surprise him/her and take them? Of course you would!

Could the favorite food of a loved one cheer them up? You bet!

Remind your loved ones of the reasons you are thankful for having them in your life. Remember with specific moments with them that make you laugh, or some of the good times they provided to you.

I know it is cliché, but think about the golden rule. If you were in this same situation, how will you like people around you to reach out and get through to you?

Ask yourself this . . . what will you miss the most about your love ones when they are not able to share this life with you anymore?

I am a firm believer that everything happens for a reason, and difficult situations are delivered in front of us for a learning purpose, a reflecting purpose, and a changing purpose.

Learning purpose—whether you are a parent, a friend, or the person in the middle of this event, life is trying to give you a message. Are you too busy and need to slow down? Are you going 100 miles per hour in the wrong direction and need to make a U turn? Are you not looking at the root cause and big picture?

Reflecting purpose—what did you do that needs some type of remedy or cure? Who did you hurt, or who hurt you that needs your forgiveness? Think about your daily routine . . . are you becoming a better version of yourself every day? What are you doing today that is helping you reach your goals? What do you need to stop doing that is keeping you from reaching those goals? Are the people in your circle of friends driving you closer to your goals, or are they pushing you farther away?

Changing or growing purpose—there is a famous quote by John C. Maxwell that reads, "Change is constant and growth is optional." Are you deciding to change something, or are you growing as you deal with all these situations coming at you from all angles? After making decisions, are you growing in your personal and professional life?

If we look at a specific situation a loved one is going through and we react by saying "They needed that so they can learn," or "I knew this will happen, but everyone learns by getting by in life," we are pushing away a valuable opportunity for us to learn. I challenge you to think, "What's the lesson I need to learn with this particular situation my friend/family member is going through right now?" "Can I do something to help them?" "What if this happens to me?"

How much trouble we will save ourselves by putting ourselves in the shoes of another person.

Many companies recommend their employees not speak in terms of "they" and "us." Management wants the employees to see themselves included and to say WE. WE are the company. I challenge YOU to think as WE when your loved ones are in difficult waters and almost drowning.

There is nothing wrong with looking for professional help, but it was my family and friends who really kept me going and helped me heal in my journey.

There is no question that my Mom and I got closer than ever during my teenage years because of this event. And my Mom and I were already pretty close; I remember going door to door selling whatever she was selling at the time (detergent, vacuums, clothing, jewelry, Avon products, and even frozen pizza at some point). It was her hard work that taught me how to be persistent in life and how to win, even when others said I couldn't.

Coming back to my goal in my new job . . . I was very focused, but I was bullied by some of the senior members of the group. They tried to tie me up with smaller and more difficult sales, which took up too much time.

Stageoflife.com discovered 91% of teens have been bullied. Bullies are put in your life to help you learn how to defeat them. By doing so, you grow in an area you haven't explored before or just didn't pay much attention to.

There is no question that some cases of bullying end in tragic events. However, I like to hear more about the good situations. The majority of those who have been bullied learn from it and take a new approach to life, often changing the way they do things for ever.

I believe someone can become more confident while dealing with this type of people. They can find a voice to speak up and learn how to deal with conflict, which will help them in college and at their future job!

My approach to my situation was about taking advantage of what I had in front of me . . . I have a slower pace sale happening which is also generating a low amount. This made my commission lower and farther away from my goal of becoming a Caribbean jewel. I'm going to treat these customers as if they were buying $3,000 worth of products. The results were surprising and almost unbelievable to every-one in the store, including the "bullies." I was turning $3-5 sales to $1,000's sales, by taking time to talk about the latest products we had available and educating the customer in special offers to take advantage of that day.

After I had turned five small amount sales into larger transactions successfully, the bullies backed off and started to respect me, even looking to me for advice to help them turn their sales into big money.

By the way, the bully in many cases is jealous of your success in academics, productivity at work, or any other skill you excel at.

Things were moving in the right direction, but my smooth ride hit major turbulence when I found out that the individual driving the other car involved in that fateful crash was stalking my work and school. I ended up in court with a protection order. So now that I had an official order from the court, everything was back to normal, correct? Well, no.

The situation was very complicated due to the other individual involved (my ex-girlfriend). You see, she went to the same school as I did, and our classes were pretty close in times and distance. Also, her place of work was directly across the hall from my store. To add more fuel onto the already engulfing fire, there was a family friend of both of them (the ex and the other driver) living in my neighborhood, which in theory gave these individuals the right to be in all 3 of the places I spent about 90% of my time.

There were conversations trying to take place to get this thing in the past and move forward with our lives. Unfortunately things took a different, more serious turn when this individual told my mom in a phone call, "I'm going to hurt your son."

It doesn't matter what the situation is: you can't tell a mom those words. How does a mother react to this kind of statement? A mother protects. My mom called the police.

When I heard what happened and the conversation my mom had with this individual, I was on fire! I wanted to do many things and it felt very much like an out-of-control situation with my arms completely tied up and no civilized solution.

My mind went in a different direction and I was making calls and having conversations with some people about maybe fixing this a different way—but there was only one problem! That's not who I am, and that's not how my parents taught me.

The police did show up, and like a Hollywood movie a quiet community turned into a scene full of cops with guns out, ready to act. At this time there was a tip that some people came with this individual inside the gated community with guns.

Nobody was harmed, and that day will be remembered as a day of disturbed peace. This could become the new normal in our family.

The last day of the month came in, and I was at $22,000. I needed $25,000 with only one hour to close the store. I remember praying, "Please let me reach this goal to WIN." The customer came in a half hour before closing. It was a long sale, and I had all the issues someone could have—from technical issues to operations issues—but the guest was very patient. The sale happened.

My goal was complete! I became a Caribbean jewel!

This was more than a goal at work. This was the first goal I was able to complete after the accident, after hearing those voices tell me, "Everything is gone and you don't have anything to live for anymore."

This was a MAJOR event in my new life of persistently reaching and surpassing goals and making dreams realities!

I want you to think of a MAJOR triumph where you reached a goal and were very proud of it.

What was it?

How did it change your life?

Chapter 5 Notes

Chapter 5 Notes

Chapter 5 Notes

CHAPTER 6

Happy Place

What's your happy place? Where would you like to be right now? When did you last discover something special that you felt would last a lifetime?

Write it down. How did you feel? What was the scene taking place? Who was part of this moment? What did you learn?

WE ALL have at least one happy place.

Before I continue, let me tell you I was not only able to WIN Caribbean Jewel in one month, I was able to repeat this two more times, making it three months in a row. This was a record for a rookie.

Things were also doing well in school and work, and the other situation was doing okay.

My cousin was getting married in Florida, and my cousins were obsessed with finding me a girlfriend. Did somebody tell them this was their duty, or did they go to "a special school" to learn how to find girlfriends for their cousins? The bride's sister (my cousin) connected me by phone with a girl from

Colombia. Before I knew it, I was talking to this girl on the phone from thousands of miles away!

I was invited to be part of my cousin's ceremony as one of the groomsmen. As significant as the wedding was for my family, nobody expected how significant this wedding would be for me.

It was a weekend in Fort Lauderdale. Nothing crazy, right?

The situation with my ex-girlfriend and the other guy was mostly under control, yet the days still were tense. There was no doubt things could escalate once again because of the proximity we all had in our daily routines to each other. My dad already had suggested to my mom that I should stay there with aunt and grandma, and although my mom never expressed this to me I knew she was thinking about it in the back of her head. Dad thought this could be a good move to calm the situation down once and for all.

We arrived in Florida. My cousin's wedding was in part possible because of the help and contribution of a church she attended, so we planned to stay in the church with everyone.

They told us the youth (I was one of those) were in the park not too far away from the church.

When I got there I was immediately captivated by the scene. A group of young people between 12-35 from many countries and backgrounds were singing and having a great time.

Have you ever had an opportunity to take part in a multicultural group of people having fun and getting along with each other?

We definitely need more of this. We all bleed the same, we are all born the same way, we are all human beings and we were all created equal.

Do you know someone that doesn't feel like they belong in their group of colleagues or in their family or even in their group of friends? Maybe this is you.

Diversity & Inclusion is an expectation more than ever, and we have a responsibility to make a difference in this world by helping others feel comfortable in their environments where they play, work, or rest.

There was definitely something different about this group. Their faces and their attitudes all felt unique, inspiring and refreshing. The way they talked with a smile was like a big family having a good time just being together.

My mind started to ask who these people were and why they were so happy. What are the requirements needed to join such a group? What other activities do they do?

This was not an AA group, yet there was a similar atmosphere where people felt the need to share their experiences with others. One of them shared the fact that he was a professional in his country and came to the United States to work many jobs including cleaning cars and picking fruits. Still he was grateful for the opportunity to work and understood others don't have this same privilege.

I continued to hear more stories and got even more impressed by the level of maturity some of the youngsters had in terms of the life they were enduring. In some cases this was a completely new place for them to call home.

I had prayed before. I went to a Christian private school for 12 years, and I did learn about singing, praying, and many other activities Christians do. I did have experiences going to church and sometimes even participated in plays and other activities in the Christian community. But the prayer I heard from a teenager at least five years younger than me, was a more powerful prayer with more humility and sincerity than I'd ever heard. These young people really liked this "Christian life," and they were not faking it just to give Mom and Dad an impression or to impress someone they like. They enjoyed it!

They didn't know me, yet they made me feel like I was family. They smiled at me, they shook my hand, they hugged me, and when I talked they listened. This was critical and is something we are losing every day.

HAPPY PLACE

We are so busy in our lives that we forget to smile. We are so consumed in our electronic devices that we are not paying attention to those who want to shake our hands. Life is passing by so fast that we forget to hug our loved ones and share affection. Our headphones are in our ears constantly, making it impossible for us to hear what others are saying.

We need the stop. Seriously, we need to STOP! We need more connections and we need more affection. We need more love and we need more hugs.

I want you to think deeply about the following questions and internalize them:

- When was the last time you hugged a family member? When is the last time you hugged yourself? Do you need a hug? Does someone in your circle of family and friends need a hug? Do an inventory in your head, and make a list of people you absolutely need to hug!

- Are you a grumpy dwarf or are you a happy one? Maybe you are completely indifferent to anything. A smile doesn't cost anything, and it is an investment with a lot of residuals. Depositing smiles on others will increase your account at the same time! Go to the mirror and smile at yourself. Take a look at that beautiful human being and give it a nice smile . . . Once again, do inventory

59

in your head and write down individuals you know need a smile and be intentional about doing it!

- Listening is the biggest action you can do to show your love and appreciation for someone. Have you ever (metaphorically) put in ear phones in order to not listen to someone? Have you felt there is really nothing you can do, so you stop listening? Do you feel it is exhausting to listen to others tell you their problems? I think that listening is something you can practice and get really good at, like a sport or hobby. Be intentional in listening to others, and I guarantee it will be very beneficial for your personal growth. You need to listen to your little voice and pay attention to moments your body is telling you do something—or NOT to do it!

Those teenagers made me feel very important. I felt very valuable and loved by people I didn't know. This was absolutely something different I was not used to seeing at all. There was something in my heart growing at this moment, something very special and spontaneous.

The activity in the park was over and we were ready to eat lunch (that's another positive thing about a multicultural group . . . Great FOOD!!).

That night I was able to experience a very similar treatment from the parents of these young teenagers. It was evident to me this was a lifestyle. The wedding was the next morning and I just couldn't wait to continue hanging out with this amazing group of people!

Ask this question to yourself right now: what's your lifestyle?

I remember in school kids use to say their lifestyle was skateboarding, surfing, or rapping. I have learned that your lifestyle is more than a sport or the type of clothing you wear. A lifestyle is all about who you are! And who you are is defined by your routine or actions you take every single day. Where do you go, what do you do, who do you hang out with? These and many more areas of your life create your lifestyle.

So I'll ask again: what's your lifestyle? Who are you? What actions do you take, and what is your routine?

Please take time to internalize these questions and dig deep into who you are.

These parents had a lifestyle that was inherited by their children (the teenagers in the park). There was something happening at home every single day for this to be possible and for the parents to have this same kind of connection with their sons and daughters.

The wedding arrived and it couldn't be more perfect, inspiring, mesmerizing and EPIC!

Interactions between me and everyone else were seamless and fitting. There were a lot of laughs and lots of moments that it felt like this place was home and these people were a part of my family. I stopped and thought: what if?

Chapter 6 Notes

Chapter 6 Notes

CHAPTER 7

The Decision

What if I can have the life of these people? What if I can behave like them? What if this is my home? Do I really feel this in me?

After the wedding was over, many of the family and church community members stayed to clean and help close down the room where it took place.

Once again I saw something special in these people. There was a sincere desire to help. Their behavior honestly took me back. Nobody was going for a prize or trophy. This was truly who they were, and how they conducted themselves in their life.

That night I stayed up thinking once again, What if? What if I live here, what if this was a calling higher than my current life, what if my life is meant to be in this place?

My life currently was in the beautiful island of Puerto Rico. I had a pretty good life, but the question came: did I feel joy and happiness? Did I truly enjoy every aspect of my life? True, I had my entire nuclear family of my mom, dad and two brothers in PR but the question remained: was I, Luis Alberto Andino Rivera, happy with my life?

I believe there are battles inside our minds, and sometimes we don't listen or don't want to listen. The best decisions we make as humans beings could be the most difficult decisions in our life. Sometimes you can't think about 'what if' with others in mind. Sometimes you can't rely on the approval of the people surrounding you. Sometimes you just have to stand tall and make the decision for the betterment of YOU . . . for the sake of improving your life and for the sake of moving forward to reach your goals.

I want you to really think about this now. When was the last time you made a life-changing decision that affected others that at the same time provided you with a happy life?

What was the situation? Who did it affect? What did you feel before and after making this decision? And how did it change your life?

That next morning and the last few days in Florida after my cousin's wedding I battled with my mind. It was like having two people inside my head: one was very excited and putting a plan together for my new life, but the other was repeating the reasons it won't work. Are you sure you want to leave your new job? You are doing so great! What about the new friends you're making, not to mention your old friends from school? What about your college classes? It will be difficult to enroll in the middle of the semester in a different place! How about your home and everything you have that is yours? You can't take all that! Are you going to leave your mom all alone, after everything she's done for you? This is how you say thank you?

When your mind is battling, there is a point where guilt sets in.

Guilt keeps people from happiness, and guilt keeps people from moving forward.

There are many people right now in a very unhappy life who won't move on because of guilt:

- The parent in an abusive relationship may stay because of the guilt of leaving the children. They believe it is better to pretend and keep children happy than moving on to a better life. They will be completely miserable and will not make the decision because they feel obligated to keep the kids happy (which they won't be anyway). Maybe this is YOU, and to you I say . . . you can't control how somebody will react to a decision you make, but you do control the actions and the integrity you hold in your own life. Living a lie is not living at all. Get out!

- The girlfriend "so in love" with her boyfriend that she will let him do whatever

he wants, including having intimate relationships with other girls with no respect
whatsoever to the commitment they made
to each other. It will only get worse. Get out!

- The husband and wife trying to live a good
life with each other who have in-laws living
in the house, trying to influence the decisions they make. You need to welcome the
advice and at the same time you can't let
others influence your decisions as a married
couple. "Thank you for the advice, we will
now move to make our decisions!"

Please read this very clearly and listen to me! DO
NOT put the responsibility of YOUR happiness in
the hands of others! You are accountable for your
own happiness and you will be disappointed and
very much unhappy if you only ever put others first.

It was my responsibility to make the best decision
for me, and it was important for me to know I had
the support of those who love me and care for me. I
was excited to tell my mom about my plan, but
obviously at first she didn't react well to this news.
She asked when will I make this move. My response
was very decisive: as soon as possible. I was feeling
energized and ready to start my new life! I just
couldn't wait!

THE DECISION

The agreement with my mom was that I would get my affairs in order. I needed to work with the college and take a look at my options. My plan was to hopefully get a transfer from my new job to Florida—which would be a pretty smooth process thanks to my Caribbean jewel. I was able to reach my goal every month I worked there, and now I had developed a successful reputation.

My manager didn't hesitate to transfer me. Though he was very sad to hear the news of me leaving, he told me he was very happy for my new journey ahead.

Things were moving forward and looking pretty good overall. It took me ten days to get things in order before I was ready to move into my new life in Florida.

The night before leaving I had a nice visit from some of my friends from high school, some of whom had been my friends for over 10 years. I felt appreciated and I felt very valued to see them take time to come and say goodbye.

We are not all parents, but I know every single one of you is a friend to somebody. A friend is probably the most critical person in a teenager's life. A friend can take a teenager to jail or to church. A friend can help you find a job or encourage you to stay at home playing games for hours. A friend can give good or bad advice. A friend can make you laugh or make you cry. Even when we are adults, a friendship is still a bonding experience we can't let go of.

How are you showing support to your friends, especially during transitional moments? Are they going into a new school? New career? New marriage? Moving to another country?

Parents, how are you showing support to your children? Do they want to move to a university thousands of miles away from home? Do they have a new boyfriend/girlfriend you are not sure about? Are they deciding to join the army? Do they want to follow a dream to be an artist or something that you may not consider a "real job?"

This world needs more people supporting and encouraging each other. You may not agree with what your loved ones are doing with their life, but it is your duty as a parent or friend to BE THERE! They need you more than you think. They need you when they are successful in their journey, and they need you when they fail and fall deeply into the abyss of life.

My mom was absolutely skeptical about my decision to move, but she was also supportive and sincere on her desire to help me achieve my goal. My dad was thrilled from the beginning—he had already suggested something similar before my trip to the wedding.

THE DECISION

The day came to get on the flight and get to my new destination—and my new life.

My mom was sad and I knew there was nothing I could do to make her feel better. It was hard knowing her sadness was a consequence of my actions. I also knew she had many doubts and concerns as to the how, the what, the where. How can she make sure I eat every day, how can she make sure I come home at night safely? What is going to be like going to a new place? What was I going to do for transportation to work? What was I going to do with school? What's going to happen when I need her and she's not there like before? Where I was going to sleep? Where I was going to work? Where is this new life going to take me?

My dad and mom arranged to meet in the airport and they both were there to say goodbye.

This was a significant point in my story because my mom and dad had a lot of baggage from when they were married. My mom suffered mistreatment by my dad, and I knew at this moment, even though they were divorced and both moved on, there was friction still. The cool thing is that my departure was bringing them together in a very special way.

The last snapshot I remember when I looked back was at both of them embracing each other while they sobbed, watching their son leave their lives to start a new one for himself.

PERSISTENT

Think about a moment in life you came together with someone you really didn't like or could not stand.

Who was it? What did they do to you? What was that moment that brought you together? What did you learn from it?

We need to make a much better effort to embrace the moments where sadness and sorrow can bring us and our enemies together.

Chapter 7 Notes

Chapter 7 Notes

CHAPTER 8

From Everything to Nothing

A flight to the unknown. The trip was a short one but the impact would be lasting, creating a series of events that changed the lives of many people. Very soon I would find out this decision was not really about me, but about what I was capable to do for others.

Like the rocking chair, life took me up and down. I almost fell by not paying attention to how fast I was going. At some moments I was very much sitting straight with my feet on the floor, secure and tight. Other times I felt like a little kid not able to reach the floor, letting the rocking chair take me on a wild journey with just a hope of not falling.

Having mom next to me to help with the fall, or having dad holding me in case I went out of control, or even looking to my brothers for support was a relief!

I had consciously and decidedly left my nuclear family behind, putting at risk the support I counted on for my entire life. I now needed to create a new support system somehow.

What now? I started to do an inventory of the things I didn't have anymore. Some would be replaced with new things, and some would need to be upgraded. I intentionally thought, "I don't have this anymore, and that's okay."

That list included:

- My nuclear family is no longer near me, though I do have my aunt, uncle, cousins, and grandparents in Florida. My aunt opened her home and I was going to stay with her family.

- I won't have my bedroom with privacy, my own things, and my own bed, but I do have a couch with a table to put my toothbrush and essentials.

- School I left behind and didn't have a similar opportunity, but I do have an opportunity to grow in other areas and create new goals.

- No car, but I do have people like my uncle and my cousin's husband to help me get to work.

- No friends, but I do have the church group that I spent time with in the park and I was excited to get to know them.

Did it suck? YES very much. Did it hurt? YES. Did I have regrets? NO. I didn't regret it at all.

I had a meeting with the District Manager in the area and he was very impressed with my Caribbean Jewel-level performance with the company so far, of which I had only been a part of for about 90 days. I knew I came with high recommendations, but soon I found out they wanted to give me the opportunity to work in one of highest-producing stores in the region (and, one could argue, the entire company). Sawgrass Mills Mall was the largest single-story outlet mall in the US. You probably recognize this name, even if you don't know much about Florida.

It was a huge privilege, and I was eager to start!

Do you remember the last time you had to change a job or transfer to a new area?

There are many variables that will keep you guessing on how this thing is going to turn out. You have new coworkers, a new area to adjust to, a new route to take to work, a new boss, and many more thoughts that may keep you up the night before.

I didn't know why or what was causing it, but I was changing. I remember thinking, "I want to do the right thing and it doesn't matter who my boss is. I will be the best I can be!"

The first day at the job felt very foreign, and like a tourist in a new country I found myself asking for directions and learning the new language. This location was very challenging because of the unique clientele coming from all parts of the world, including South America, Asia, and Europe. It was a very fast-paced environment, and there was a new way I needed to learn in order to keep up. In my old store, it was all about taking time and really digging in the needs of the guest by being thorough. Here, in my new location, it was about how quickly you can finish with one customer and move on to the next one.

What did I do to find success in my new job with new clientele and a new pace of selling? I created a balance between the way I was used to doing things and the new way I was learning. I observed very closely what the others did, and took specific practices to help me get better. I asked for help, and followed the directions I was taught.

It is my personal belief that some people are not good at asking for help because of multiple reasons:

1. They are afraid people will think they don't know something and don't want to be seen as someone who is naïve. Someone once said "the only stupid question is that one you don't ask." It is better to ask and get clarification and understanding rather than to keep doing it wrong because you feel it will be dumb to ask.

2. They are too proud to ask. Some people are suffocated by pride, which keeps them from moving forward and experiencing new things. You can always learn, from everyone you meet. You can learn things from a five-year-old, you can learn things from teenagers, and you can learn things from adults. Always learning from people, no matter their age, will keep your work relevant in this age of technology and innovation.

3. They don't see the need to ask because they think they know pretty much everything. Some people simply believe they know more. They don't think they could possibly learn something from others that are in a lower position/status compared to them.

Regardless of the reason, you are never so knowledgeable to stop learning, and if you believe that you are, I can see your problem already. Learning never stops. You have to open your mind to learn something every day.

It has been only four months since I had the accident, only four months since I had a true desire to not be in this world. There is a new sense of accomplishment and excitement in my new life. Yes, there are many things I do not have and there are many things changing. This is probably the biggest life transition I will ever make, and it has been scary, uncertain, and very stressful. At the same time, I felt I had come to grasp something I had completely lost four months ago, and perhaps was missing in my daily life even before that accident: Peace!

I would go to work in a car that was borrowed from my uncle . . . and I had Peace!

I would get to my aunt's house where I only had a toothbrush and a few essentials . . . and I had Peace!

This place was nothing like my home in Puerto Rico where I could enter my room, close the door, and not to be bothered for hours . . . and I had Peace!

I couldn't call my mom or spend time with her . . . and I had Peace!

My friends were far away and I couldn't text them to meet in the court to play basketball . . . and I had Peace!

I was changing. There was something in me driving me to think differently. At the same time, it gave me a Peace I hadn't felt ever before in my young life.

What's your definition of Peace? What needed to happen in your life for you to receive and feel Peace?

FROM EVERYTHING TO NOTHING

Maybe something needed to stop for you to have a peaceful time or you needed to change environments.

I want you to take this moment to think about your quest toward Peace. What does that look like?

Let me give you some perspective about what Peace was for me:

- Peace was for me to go to bed and sleep well without having to worry about the screams and physical fights between my parents. This was a tough time in my life as a kid.

- It was going through a month or year without having an episode where my hypoglycemia attacks injured my body and made me faint or feel really sick.

- It was going in the car with my family and not having to worry about my dad scream- ing at others because of angry driving behavior, putting his family at risk with his actions.

- Peace was knowing I could go to the park and play with my friends without worrying about older kids coming to bother and bully us.

Whether you are a teenager, young adult, adult or parent, probably you identify yourself with some of these.

With all that being said, the Peace I was feeling was not based on others' actions and it wasn't based on something I did or didn't do. The Peace I was feeling came from another place. This peace didn't feel temporary or something that would be over soon. This felt like a lasting, real, and tangible Peace.

How's this possible, you ask? How can someone with nothing find Peace? Where is this peace coming from, and how can you feel it too?

These questions will be answered in the next chapters.

Right now, I want you to think about your actions and how you can help others find some peace.

Think about this: do you know of anything you are doing that is disturbing the peace of someone else?

I'm not talking about loud music. I'm talking about a specific behavior you do or don't do that causes a lack of peace in someone else.

Think deeply and do a personal inventory on your life. Start with those close to you, your wife/ husband, kids, parents, family overall, coworkers, friends, neighbors and more.

FROM EVERYTHING TO NOTHING

After my mom and dad got separated, my brothers and I found ourselves in a very not peaceful home. They thought it was better to be together, and they didn't realize their separation while staying in the same house compromised the peace we had as a family. I remember having conversations with my dad when I was still in middle school, where I told him it was better to see him leave the house.

I want you to write down what you need to start doing to provide a peaceful life for others, as well as what will you need to *stop* doing.

I challenge you to think about the most important thing in your life—and whether you ask for a vacation or some time to unwind and relax, that is your Peace!

Chapter 8 Notes

Chapter 8 Notes

Chapter 8 Notes

CHAPTER 9

The Light at the End of the Tunnel

Changing a habit is not easy, and moving on from an addiction is even harder. Some people find success in taking small steps, and for some it works to start with a goal. Usually, it's best to start with accepting there is a problem that needs fixing.

In order to change a habit, you must take action.

Another way to change a habit is to have an accountability partner, someone you can trust who will keep you honest in your goal and will help you achieve it by reminding you of the commitment you have made.

The method I use to change a habit is "replacement." This means I will start by replacing the time I spent doing one thing with doing something else. For example, listening to music. Maybe I replace that time I spent in the car listening to music with listening to TED talks or inspiring podcasts.

Maybe instead of watching TV when I come home from work, I take that time to read a book or work on a special project.

I was starting a new life, and I needed new changes and new goals to keep me on point.

Are you reviewing your goals every week and checking on your progress?

I believe many times we see people not reaching their goals because either they are not clear on what they are and don't understand how to achieve them, or they do know but don't follow up and track progress. It is important that you adjust as needed in the journey to reach and surpass your goals.

My goals consisted of three areas:

1. I needed new friends and wanted to establish new relationships with people that will make me better. One of the biggest mistake people do, especially young people, is to hang out with the wrong crowd. We have all heard our moms asking who we are hanging out with. Choosing your friends carefully could make a huge difference in your life now and in the future.

   Think about these questions, and if any of them are yes you may have good friends: Do your friends hold you accountable for your goals? Do they visit you when you are sick, or call you to let you know they are thinking about you? Do they give you advice on how to respect your parents and loved ones? Do they know some of your favorite things, like your favorite food, movie, place to vacation? Maybe it's time to review some of your friendships to think about how good they are for you and the achievements you want to accomplish.

2. I needed a new support system, and it doesn't necessarily have to do with friends directly. There are people in our lives that we trust with a conversation about the desires in our heart. My grandma became one of those great people to talk to and ask for guidance. My cousin's husband became another person that I trusted with work-related issues, like difficult conversations with coworkers and colleagues. Some parents from church were very good at providing advice, whether it was about a career move or a love life decision. Ask yourself again: do you have a support system? If not, can you think of two or three people that can become your support system?

3. I needed to set goals and implement them successfully. Everyone has new ideas every day, and only those that write it down are taking action about it. Some do not only write it down, they move into

implementation phase. I had many ideas on how to help my colleagues be more productive at work and how to help my manager make the experience better for our customers. Many times your ideas and implementation will get you closer to a promotion, career move, or professional/personal goal. In my case I was promoted to assistant manager within months of starting this new job. Do you have any ideas that are in your head? Put them on paper! Do you have them on paper? Put them into action! Do you have any implemented that are not doing well? Review your plan and tweak it as needed to re-launch it and execute!

My life was getting back in shape with these three important elements moving forward and leveraging the opportunities in front of me.

At this point I had multiple things going in the right direction. I felt like a well-oiled machine—running smoothly with no hiccups.

I was actively participating in the youth group at our church and I was very much involved in outreach programs and other things to help me give back to the community and other people that needed it the most. There were very good friends I made already in church, and I learned so much about opportunities I was given that others couldn't have because of their place of birth. I was considered an American citizen because I was born in Puerto Rico, but I made friends that came from other countries that unfortunately didn't have the same opportunities Puerto Ricans have. I was ignorant about the hard work and the obstacles someone from another country goes through compared to people born with American citizenship.

Think about a time where you were ignorant in something. After you were enlightened, it gave you a perspective about life that changed the way you saw things moving forward. Some people are born in a town and don't know what it's like going to live in the city. Some people are not aware of how hard it is to be a parent until they become one. Some people are completely oblivious of the consequences of their lifestyle. The reality is that we are ignorant in almost everything until we decide to make an effort to learn more about it.

At work, things were moving along with my promotion to assistant manager, and I soon had the opportunity to participate in a larger class of people wanting to jump their career to a manager role. Wow, *manager*! I couldn't believe I was thinking of doing this. I was only 19 years old and this sounded like such a big step for me.

I still remember receiving my binder. It weighed over 20 pounds and contained the entire curriculum of becoming a "manager." There were over

30 people in the class and I remember thinking it would be a tough task. Some of this people had worked for the company for years, and I had not been there for even one full year yet. I felt I would probably be the last person in my class to become a manager.

Do you remember a time you were given an opportunity to showcase yourself against others? Maybe you are dealing with this right now. Are you in a place where you feel your goal is going to take a long time to reach?

Let me share with you a couple thoughts about opportunities and how they may go:

1. Have confidence in yourself. I don't know what they will offer you. All I know is that they don't have you. You can think about what everyone else has, but it doesn't matter. They are not YOU!

2. Identify the group you know is serious about the task at hand and try to get connected with them. Exchange phone numbers and emails to create a network for future references, including in areas you will like to improve that they maybe mastered.

3. Be an overachiever. If there is a deadline to complete a specific task, do it in less time. You want to establish yourself as above average. Commit to do it better and quicker.

4. Ask for feedback from your teacher or others in your same situation. In my case, I reached to other managers I knew had my best interest at heart. I also could have asked someone who was considered an expert to review some of my assignments or tasks to make sure I was on point.

5. Finish the class, task, workshop, homework or whatever it is you are trying to accomplish. Tell yourself no matter what happens, I will get it done. Many people fail in their commitments because they don't have a sense of urgency. No matter the circumstances, do not change your commitments.

Don't be afraid to take on multiple tasks and improve yourself in a particular area. YOU CAN.

My life at home was doing pretty good as well. I still didn't have my own room, or privacy, but that would not last much longer.

Patience is a virtue. The best things in life are those that come after you were patiently waiting and hoping they would become a reality.

I had momentum going in my life and things were happening almost simultaneously with many opportunities presenting themselves without me looking for them.

Don't get desperate about a promotion. If you are working hard and doing not only what you been asked but even a bit more, things will get better and you will get promoted! Be patient.

If you feel there is a dark time in your love life and things are not looking good overall, do not get anxious. Stay focused on your life and don't *try* to find love. Many times, you just need to wait and be patient. Love will find YOU!

Do you see the light at the end of the tunnel? Do you see things getting better?

Think about a time you felt things were not good and you waited patiently to see results. Those results came at the time you needed, to help you be in the place you needed to be.

It has been just over six months since the accident. My life was about to elevate to new heights I could not even dream of.

My mom had achieved her own level of accomplishments as well, after persistently going after her dreams. She went to college while taking care of three sons. Through this, she worked a full time job and a second job making cakes and cookies to pay for her school. She's an example of how you can succeed by being persistent in reaching your goals.

THE LIGHT AT THE END OF THE TUNNEL

She proceeded to earn her college degree and reach the highest goals in her bakery business.

Chapter 9 Notes

Chapter 9 Notes

Chapter 9 Notes

CHAPTER 10

Milestone of Firsts

Think about the many firsts you have had so far in your life, and contemplate the moment they took place.

Do you remember your first steps? Probably not, but your parents do. Your mom, I guarantee, still has the shoes you wore when this event took place. It was certainly a special moment, and it will continue to be for all the new families out there.

How about your first kiss? I can certainly tell you who and where! I was five years old, it was on my birthday, and her name was Ana. The stomach gets all twisted and you feel the so called butterflies in your belly.

How about the first time your parents let you go on your bike to the store for bread? This was not only a major milestone for you. Your parents also felt the anxiety. Maybe they even gave you a walkie-talkie. I rode my bike to Mr. Jose's store on street #4 of my neighborhood. As I'm pedaling my way out of home and I look back to contemplate and appreciate the responsibility I was just given felt empowering. This type of event is a big deal for any kid.

First time driving your parents' car? Do you remember the model and year? Do you remember the thrilling excitement you felt? Mine was a Toyota Camry 1988 and a Ford pickup 1997. How many times did I go around the block so excited it felt like I just took it on the highway?

First game system is easy to know—you probably disappeared for days when you got yours. Some of us think there was a conspiracy against children by parents to not let them go outside, but it was the kids not wanting to go out because they had Nintendo.

First camping trip—maybe it wasn't something that thrilling to you, but I remember it was just to the east of Puerto Rico's coast. The beach was our shower, wild-caught fish was the food, and play time meant using natural resources in the midst of a camp fire.

First drink? In Puerto Rico you can start drinking at 18, and on my 18th birthday I asked my dad to take me to Chili's for a not-virgin-anymore Pina colada. After 1 sip I had my first and my last alcoholic drink in my lifetime.

First paycheck—is one of the first moments in life you truly appreciate how hard your parents work to give you the things you have. I was 16, working in a super market as a bagger and making just a little over $4 per hour. I was super excited to see over $40 after working 2 weeks. The feeling of seeing that piece of paper with your name on it . . . priceless!

First car-The first car is either the one that went through Mom, Dad, or your older brothers or is a car bought just for you. Either way, it was exhilarating to see this Nissan Sentra of 1985 with holes in the chassis! I didn't care about what it looked like! It was *my car*!

First time you were in "love." I'm not sure if we can call those relationships we had in school "love." Now that I'm older, I could say with certainty it was more of an infatuation. I remember two particular girls in middle school time, one started with letter L . . . and the other with letter R . . .

First day of high school, first day of college, first day staying outside your home and many, many more firsts in life give you shape as you grow and make your life come to form.

I was about to experience many firsts. They all came within a six-month period and all held promise to elevate life to a new level of accomplishment and excitement, I set new goals to reach and surpass.

My first experience in a youth retreat, I was initially unable to go because the collection of money had passed and the spaces were completely full. Remember those friends from Chapter 6? They helped me get in and took care of me while I was there as well.

I was in awe to see many people with the same type of attitude, smiles, energy, and testimonies like my friends when I got to the park just months before. Little did I know in this camp, I would meet the best thing humanly possible that could happen to someone. My partner in life, my friend for eternity, my wife!

The story is a little more complicated. There was a girl that impressed me and touched my heart with her testimony, energy, enthusiasm, and simply how happy she looked.

After listening to her testimony that night I was persistent on finding her somehow. It was dark and I was with a friend with flashlights when we heard two girls singing. Their voices were beautiful! I recognized the girl from earlier and I just started to talk to her while my friend talked to the other girl.

The next day I was looking for her and couldn't find her, but I did find her friend. We literally went in on a journey through the campgrounds. We ended up sitting and watching a competition on the lake.

The next day, we exchanged numbers. We kept in contact throughout the next months and really formed a friendship. The girl from the testimony that I was impressed with became someone I started to like more and more. Her friend and I also had conversations. This friend gave me advice on things the girl liked and how to impress her. One day we even planned a surprise together where I was able to meet them to hang out without the girl knowing.

Have you ever been really focused on one thing? Have you ever put so much of your effort on making something happen that you forget the things life wants to give you?

I want you to think about a time where you were persistent on something and it just didn't quite get there. A time when it almost seemed like life was saying, "Do not go there. I have something else."

What was this thing you wanted so badly? What did you learn? What would you change, if anything about this experience?

Well, I was persistent in my relationship with this girl, and I really enjoyed picking her up in the car of my dreams to go out dinner.

Wait, I didn't tell you about the car of my dreams?!

Allow me to go back a couple of months to right after I received my promotion to assistant manager. Years earlier, I had seen my older brother renting a car for his graduation. This car instantly became the car I wanted to have one day, even though at the time I thought I would have to be like 40 to have a stable job making enough money for such a good car. This car was again rented for my middle brother, and we rented one for my graduation as well. I even rented one for my ex-girlfriend's graduation (the one from the car accident).

The point is, having this car was a dream. I wouldn't have ever imagined my dream would come to life almost simultaneously with my first promotion.

My Ford Mustang, bright red, everything about this car was exciting! And when I found out there was a possibility of me achieving this goal so soon it was exhilarating. *Fueling.*

Now, this was the first car I was going to buy brand-new with 0 miles. My company would give me a discount, which was such a great opportunity I couldn't let it go. I found out very quickly the cost of having a sports car was mind boggling.

Once I was in the dealership, everything seemed to go to plan. I was set to pay about $270 per month for this car after discounts and all the great deals I received. I was good to go, but then that word . . . that terrible word . . . (Horror music in the back ground) *insurance*! No, wait, what, NO!!!! The payment for the insurance was more than the car payment!! A 19-year-old in a brand new mustang screams higher insurance payment!

MILESTONE OF FIRSTS

Do you remember your first new brand-new car? Or do you have a dream car that is your goal?

What was/is it? What color?

At this point I was so persistent on getting the car and completing my goal that I said to myself I would figure something out. This is when I started a process that would change the way I did things at work.

In order for me to pay for the car and the insurance, I needed to create a plan to make at least 35% more than what I was currently getting. The cool thing was that I worked sales, and I was able to make uncapped commission. I created a calculator to help me track my sales based on the hours I worked, giving me a clear understanding of where would I be at any given time of the day, week, and month to achieve my goals.

This is the first time I created a tool to help me accomplish the goals I had. It was out of necessity, but this tool would later be used nationally in all the stores in our company by all members.

Have you ever created a tool to help you accomplish your goals, personally and professionally?

What did you create? Did you share it with others? Do you see the value still today? Do you use it today?

PERSISTENT

I was able to accomplish my goals and pay for my car and insurance comfortably.

Achieving your goals is important. We all need to keep an inventory of what we are setting ourselves up to do and what we are doing right now to help us get there.

Do you have any firsts in life that you would like to accomplish? Set up a date. No, really, let's do it right now.

Write down below at least one "first" you want to accomplish this year—or even in the next few months:

By this date _____ I will accomplish this goal _____.

Do you want to go on vacation to a place you have never been before? Maybe you have never taken a cruise or gone on an airplane.

Maybe you want to take a class to better yourself in a specific area, like cooking. Maybe you want to bake your first cake, or grill something outside for the first time.

How about buying your first brand-new car? Or going to a youth camp, or couples retreat?

Maybe this goal is something as simple as going on a hike, or doing one hour of cardio, or waking up earlier to pray and meditate.

MILESTONE OF FIRSTS

I encourage you to reach many first this year. I also encourage you to keep inventory of what you accomplished and what you have yet to accomplish!

There is no doubt that in less than six months my life turned around 360 degrees (maybe even more like 720). It was not done yet!

There would be another tragedy that would touch the world and affect everyone's routine—and in doing so, it put my goals in a very fragile situation.

Chapter 10 Notes

Chapter 10 Notes

Chapter 10 Notes

CHAPTER 11

Dreams Coming True

The day the country stood together nothing . . . NOTHING was the same ever again. I vividly remember turning on the TV, getting prepared to go to work.

They showed images of an airplane hitting one of the twin towers in New York, and there was an instant confusion and desperation. As I got in the car and started driving the second plane hit the second tower. Now we knew there was a bigger problem.

I mentioned earlier that I worked in one of the biggest, busiest malls in the nation. That day when I arrived, it was evident how lonely the halls connecting over a mile of stores would be. There was a threat, and we had police checking garbage cans and sweeping the entire mall for anything suspicious.

Where were you during September 11? Do you remember your reaction?

PERSISTENT

I remember feeling furious anger—and at the same time, a sense of not being able to do anything.

That week I remember going to a friend's house to study the history of our country versus others that didn't like us very much. I was very naïve about the fact that there were places in the world that truly hated our people. That was very difficult to swallow.

This would not be an ordinary month. People were too scared to even show up to window shop.

Here it is the question that haunted me for days: What can I do to make it better? How can I share love and hope in the middle of this mess?

I had a renewed desire to deliver a great experience to whoever came through the door.

Many of my co-workers were looking for ways to create additional income because the mall was not busy at all. It was a difficult time to be a salesperson who got paid on commission.

Because of my persistent attitude and the that fact many local customers were coming back to see me and make purchases, I was able to have a good month in October in comparison to peers not only in my own store but in other locations across the district and region.

There was a report measuring all the assistant managers and managers-in-training for the entire district and region. The report from October put me in the top 2 candidates to be a manager out of over thirty at the time.

There was a big lesson to learn about the unfortunate events of September 11 and its aftermath. I know many individuals that showed resiliency and refocused themselves on making a big difference in their job, home, and community. This gave the world hope that there was good in humanity, and people will make an effort to make the world a better place for those coming after us.

Those people received a job or lifetime opportunity in a very difficult time because of how they dealt with one of the most challenging times in their life.

It is not how you handle yourself in the good times when everything is marching well. It is about what attitude you represent when things are going the other way. It is about what solutions you can bring to the table to make it better. As JFK once said, "Ask not what your country can do for you, but what can you do for your country."

The quote is about responsibility and account-ability. Are you holding yourself accountable every single day? Are you doing an inventory of your goals to reflect on your actions and match with your progress to reach those goals?

Please take time to think about a specific trouble at work or at home where you blamed everything and everyone but you.

What was the situation?

Now, think about how that situation would have gone if you took ownership and found a solution instead of pointing fingers.

Let me give you a simple example. A 16-year-old comes home and tells her parents she's pregnant. As devastating as this is for the parents and as much as the girl is to blame for her decisions, this is not the time to scream at her—and it is *never* the time to be physically aggressive.

My advice is to stop and think: what is the other person going through, and what is their state of mind? Let's take a look at this from the 16-year-old's point of view. Probably about one month ago she found out that she was pregnant. Maybe the father wants to take responsibility, maybe not. She's trying to get advice from multiple people outside her home on how to deliver the news to Mom and Dad. She pictures in her head over and over coming home with Mom in the kitchen and Dad watching TV. She pictures herself walking in with her head down and shameful body language, speaking the words "I'm pregnant." Over and over she pictured the different reactions they would have and next steps she would take based on those reactions. One of those steps is leave the home, or worse.

I can speak about this because I had the opportunity to counsel many young people, including teenagers, in the nonprofit organization I support.

Grandparents, this is the first time your grandson or granddaughter is in your life and you want to celebrate by screaming at him/her? Stop and think about how critical this moment is in your daughter's life . . . She needs you more than EVER before! This is the type of unconventional reaction/attitude we need in this world to make it a better place.

You can be persistent on loving your daughter so much that it doesn't matter what she is doing or did; you will understand she needs you more than anything else.

Because of how I handled this challenging situation, I was able to create a new opportunity. My attitude showed people hope. My reaction showed people that nothing is impossible when you are focused and engaged actively in reaching your goals.

Within months of this event I would be given an opportunity to reach one of my dreams.

The Dream: becoming a manager of my own store. To run my business and support all employees working. The amount of responsibility given to someone in this position was great, and it did not come without many challenges. At 20 years old with no college diploma, on the month of April

2002 I had reached a goal that only I could dream of. I was one of the youngest managers in the company out of over 4000 storefronts.

The class of 30 dropped and only a few got to finish the class, with only a couple making it to the actual management milestone. Some took a shortcut in the tough times, and their decisions to compromise integrity took them to fall from the company.

Don't take shortcuts. You may get away with it at the beginning, but there is someone always watching, including when you are alone.

Shortcuts will only take you to a life of disappointments and regrets. You will give others you love a reason to weep and sorrow. There will be a part of you that you will not be able to repair, and if you do want to repair it, it can take time, resources, your credibility, your integrity, and your honesty. Rebuilding those would be the most challenging thing you can ever do. I see people who take shortcuts lose their job for pennies on the dollar and have to come home to tell their family. I see people taken to jail, losing their future of going to school to be a doctor or lawyer in a split second.

Don't do it! Wait, and do the right thing. As one of my inspirational leaders Tim (an executive in the company I work) always says, "The good guys always win."

So, do you remember a time where you took a shortcut, only to regret it almost immediately?

What was it? What lesson did you learn? What advice will you give to someone thinking about taking a shortcut?

Everything was going pretty well at work and I was about to make another dream come true!

It happened in the parking lot of my store. She came to bring me a piece of my favorite dessert (tres leches). I was helping customers and saw her coming into the store with a nice smile. I finished my conversation with my customers and we came outside to talk in the parking lot. I was thanking her for bringing my favorite dessert, and when we said goodbye there was a very special moment and we both felt a connection.

Let me go back a little . . . in this youth camp over a year ago, I had the opportunity to meet two girls who were best friends. I went out with the one I liked to eat, and there were activities we shared during this time. In the meantime, I had conversations with her friend, Sara, about how to impress her best friend. We (Sara and I) became very close friends.

I remember having a conversation with my grandma about the girl I wanted in my life, and I started describing and going over certain qualities. She had to be compassionate, love to be with people, love her parents, have a good foundation of values, active in church and her community. At some point my grandma stopped me and made me realize I was literally describing Sara, the friend of the girl I (thought I) liked.

How was it possible I didn't see this before? Sara was probably having some of those questions in her mind and heart as well. The incident in the parking lot was not coincidence. It was the new reality of where things were going.

While all this was happening, I had a trip scheduled to Las Vegas after winning a contest for having one of the highest performing locations in the region of the company.

It's funny. I was going to Las Vegas which I have never been to before, but all I could think of was my relationship with her and where this journey was heading.

I was in the top of the stratosphere having a conversation with her. Before and after the shows, I was on the phone with her. It was as if she was there with me, and I could certainly feel her in my heart and mind. I couldn't stop thinking about her and our relationship.

As I was getting prepared to go back home I had the craziest idea. I needed to plan it perfectly.

I was on the plane and on the phone with a flower shop, trying to order some flowers before the plane took off so they would be there when I arrived. I had the attention of everyone in the plane, and they started saying "Aww . . ."

I asked Sara to meet me in the Dolphin Mall, our preferred meeting destination due to the proximity between our homes. I arrived in Florida and my heart was pumping really fast, I knew what I wanted to do and how I wanted to do it, but still I was sweating inside.

I picked up the flowers, a Lindt chocolate bar, and a card that said "You complete me." We met close to where my car was. At this moment my mind was blank and I was so nervous. She knew something was up.

I said something like this: "I was in Las Vegas and all I could think about was YOU and US." At this moment I gave her the chocolate, card, and flowers. "I feel very comfortable when I'm around you and you bring something into my life that I don't have. Will you be my girlfriend?"

She said YES!

Starting a new relationship is very special. There is an excitement very difficult to describe. Some people use butterflies to attempt to share how they feel during this moment.

PERSISTENT

In a period of less than four months, I reached the highest potential in my professional life by taking awards for top store in the District and Region. I had one of the highest performing locations in the Nation. I was living the dream, traveling to destinations like Dallas, Las Vegas & New Mexico.

And now, my personal life was taking a new height with someone I knew was a blessing and would continue to be a blessing in my life.

Today, we have been happily married for thirteen years and have two beautiful, healthy boys. However, even though she is someone I love very much and treasure like no other human being, she wasn't my one true love.

Chapter 11 Notes

Chapter 11 Notes

CHAPTER 12

Finding my
One True Love

Rewind back to the night I had the accident that led me into the darkest period of my life.

After the accident, I attempted to take my own life many times. I tried to intentionally harm myself to a point of making death a reality. It was incredible how I was able to endure these actions and yet repeat attempts to fulfill my dark desire at the same time.

I didn't know it then, but someone else had bigger plans for me . . . someone else was watching everything from a distance. I believe everything happens for a reason, and GOD has His reasons.

Many times we like to question the reason why our lives turn out the way they do. We think, "Why me?" Well, the answer is because you are special, and this could be a needed trial to make you stronger, better, and smarter for incoming bigger trials. Maybe God lets you suffer today because he can see how happy you will be tomorrow.

PERSISTENT

My persistent attitude is not coming from a human place. This is an act of heaven. The Bible says, "I can do all things in Christ that gives me strength." (Philippians 4:13)

Going to the park that day with those young people and seeing them with a glow in their face was all part of His plans. He told me that day in my mind: this is what I have for you. I will give you happiness, and you will smile more. This glow is yours as well. He spoke to me that day, and I listened.

My motivation to leave everything I had was not just a change of life but a change of lifestyle guided by the creator of the universe. He called me and I heard with actionable ears and body. I didn't just listen, I acted!

The creator of the universe had interest in me. He knows my name, He knows how many hairs I have on my head, He knows my sorrows, He knows my weakness, He knows my happy place, and He had a beautiful plan for my life.

After the day in the park, I was ready to take part in more activities like those. I couldn't wait for the next day in church to participate. When I came to my new life, I was excited about work and I was anxious about many other things. Still my mind was in that day in the park, and the experiences after that in the wedding and reception were with everyone from the church.

God used this youth group and the church to make me realize hope, peace, and love are as real as the accident I had. I will find very quickly all three of them in this church and in the people.

I wanted more. I wanted more and more. What's the next step and what do I need to do? God called me again, and I responded. He called me to take action and tell the world He is the love of my life, and I will surrender everything I have to him. In March 2001, in the pool of one of the most beautiful, caring families I ever met before, I got baptized. It was like no other feeling I had ever felt or will ever feel again. I was saying goodbye to my old life and welcoming my new life in Christ! Old things were in the past, and new things were on their way.

In less than six months I went from not wanting to be in this world to needing to do more in this world. I have so much to offer, and with God in me, who can be against me?

I was born again!

Everything came as a result of my decision to give my life completely to the Lord. EVERYTHING!

He's been calling me for a long time, and He let me fall into the lowest ground so when I looked up his gratuitous mercy and power could be seen clearly.

I was developing new habits and saying goodbye to the old. I had a new focus on the things He had in store for me.

Probably one of the biggest things in my life is music. It changes the way I think and behave, so I took a stand and committed to only listen to uplifting music that would help me grow to be a better person. The music I listened to in my previous life was degrading to my development as young individual and a threat to the person I wanted to become.

You are what you listen to, so I was passionate about only listening to uplifting music. Everyone needed to get used to the fact that if they got in my car, they had to prepare to be uplifted with positive messages coming from my radio.

I'm not sure what your status is, or what you are listening to right now, but I challenge YOU with this question: Is the music you listen to helping you get closer to the person you want to be?

I was focused on changing my lifestyle and I knew I needed to start with music. Because of this decision in my life, I was able to inspire others to do the same. Now there are testimonies of young people who made the same decision saying, "I sleep better now, I can concentrate more at school, I have more enthusiasm for learning and development," and many others.

FINDING MY ONE TRUE LOVE

I'm not here to judge anyone. The purpose of this book is to challenge the life you are currently leading and ask yourself, "Could I be persistent on giving my life an upgrade?" Probably, and it's probably a much-needed upgrade!

Think about this . . .

Do you want to be a better athlete? Maybe a better basketball player or a soccer player?

What habits are you doing today that are keeping you from achieving your goal? What do you need to replace with new habits in order to get closer to your goals and dreams? Maybe it is as simple as having less screen time.

Maybe you want to be a better father or mother. What bad habits are you replacing with good habits? Maybe it is giving healthier food to your kids. Maybe it is developing a schedule to make sure you have 30 minutes a day of uninterrupted fun time with them. I'm not talking about regular things you need to do like bathing or taking them to sleep, I'm talking about time for just laughing and enjoying each other.

Maybe you just want to be better overall for your husband or wife? Maybe dedicate a special time in the week to hang out. Maybe do a smaller activity with them every day, like eating breakfast together, praying together, or reading together. I do recommend you stay away from any type of screen.

The cool thing is that when you are doing things with the help of a higher power, everything becomes easier. EVERYTHING!

Having God by your side is like having a superhero next to you at all times. Life is a bully, and we need God to show life and our enemies that we are not alone. With His help, anything is possible.

If God is with you, then nothing can come against you. NOTHING!

I accepted God in my heart and surrendered my life to him. I never thought I could have done it, but I did, and I KNOW *YOU* CAN, TOO!

He took charge in my life. Things became way better once I began obeying his plan in my life and let go of my ways. I learned that HIS ways were higher, better, and just amazing!

Do you ever feel lonely? Do you ever feel like something is missing? Do you ever feel like maybe you don't have a purpose, or you are just going through the motions? Many people in this world feel the same way. I am a firm believer that these feelings develop because deep in our soul we long to have a relationship with our Creator. There is a part missing in all of us, and we are looking for it in the wrong places.

Have you ever heard of stories where kids are looking for their fathers and mothers? They are doing everything they can to find this relationship. Some parents are basically business transactions in those donor banks. Sometimes people are adopted. Children in both of these scenarios grow and at some point have questions about their birth parents.

At this point the parents in their life have a choice. My experience is that they always tell their kids the truth. Here is where these stories become fascinating, even though they never knew their father or mother from birth and even though they don't even know what they look like. There is a desire and a passion to get to know them and spent time with them! Why is that? Why will people go so far to find someone who, for many years or even their entire life, has been missing? Well, the answer is simple. They have a connection that nobody else has or will ever have. Mother and father from birth helped make that special individual and we are all created equal in this regard! ALL!

Like the mother and father from birth, God is a sovereign creator and the maker of all things—including every single human being. We belong to Him, and we have a special connection with Him!

We need Him. We need Him more than we can ever imagine. A human being will not be able to feel complete until they start a relationship with Him!

Maybe you are a religious person and maybe you go to church every week. Maybe there is something missing in your life, a lonely place you come to every night, a void you can't understand. I will challenge you to rethink your relationship with God.

Jesus said, "I give you peace." This is not like how the world gives peace. The ACTUAL, truthful peace is feeling free from everything and understanding God is in control. Your health is in His control, your financials are in His control, your marriage is in His control, your kids are in His control, and everything you have is in His control!

There is no other peace like the one given by our Creator! Do you currently enjoy the benefits of true peace? I invite you to learn more about Him and this great peace He offers to you.

Just remember this, he's a gentleman and he will not take control if you don't allow him to. Jesus said, "I'm here at the door, I Call and if someone hears and opens the door I will come in and have dinner with them." He calls, and WE need to answer and voluntarily open the door.

I'm alive because of God's mercy. I'm here sharing this with you because He has completely changed my life.

Not everything is perfect and it will never be. Don't think for a minute that giving your heart to God will take issues away and everything will just disappear. It doesn't work that way.

Think about any class you ever taken. There was a lecture from the teacher and there were also actions you needed to take. Whether it was homework or studying for a test, you needed to be prepared at all times. The key word here is <u>action</u>.

<u>Every single day we need to give God control of our lives.</u>

<u>There are 3 specific ways the Bible teaches us how to do this:</u>

1. **Talk to Him every single day as much as you can through prayer and meditation.**

2. **Read testimonies and lessons He has given everyone throughout the life-time of this world. Read the Bible.**

3. **Take care of others like they were your brothers and sisters. Teach them the things you learn. Share your testimony, and you will help others transform their lives.**

A relationship with God is not a "religion" thing, but more of a "common sense" thing.

I believe God was persistent in reaching out to me in many ways. Sometimes He let things happen, even tragic events that really hurt in my life, but at the end it is all about us turning to Him and accepting we need our Creator every day in our lives.

He is calling you today, and He will continue to be persistent in pursuing a relationship with you. What will you do?

Chapter 12 Notes

Chapter 12 Notes

Acknowledgements

To the Creator of all things, my heavenly Father, who gifts me with the strength and clear mind to be a better human being every day.

To my wife, Sara, for her absolute support and encouragement to start and finish this work.

I'd like to thank my mom, Iris Rivera, for her support and contribution with many phone calls trying to keep this story accurate; a mom who is always there no matter the distance.

My dad, Luis A. Andino, for his support and for being there when I need him.

My grandmother, Mercedes Colon, and my late grandfather, Justino Rivera, for their persistence in trying to keep our family closer to God.

My nieces, Natalie and Shedialis Andino, for giving their feedback and help create a work for all teenagers and parents to enjoy. My nephew, Enrique Andino, for doing a great job with my photo.

PERSISTENT

My aunt, Mercedes Hernandez, and her late husband, Joy, for taking me in and helping me with the transition to a new life.

My cousin, Meradie, and her husband, Esteban, for their support and helping me get to work on time. My cousin, Meraida, for making me laugh and making my transition a fun one.

My uncle, Justino (Junior), for his support during the transition and letting me borrow his car.

My friends from the Margate SDA Church in Florida for helping me become a better person by showing me how to build relationships, keep a humble attitude, and serve others in anything you can.

Special thanks to the following families for welcoming me into their homes: La Verde, Sanchez, Broncano-Jacome, Candelier, Ortiz, Gonzalez, Gutierrez-Perlaza, Arboleda, Vazquez, Feitosa, Pitti, Martinez, Rios, Taborda, Añez, Nuñez, Bernhardt, Torres, Pabon and to every member of these families.

NOW IT'S YOUR TURN

**Discover the EXACT 3-step blueprint you need
to become a bestselling author in 3 months.**

Self-Publishing School helped me, and now I want
them to help you with this FREE WEBINAR!

Even if you're busy, bad at writing, or don't know
where to start, you CAN write a bestseller
and build your best life.

With tools and experience across a variety of niches and
professions, Self-Publishing School is the only resource
you need to take your book to the finish line!

DON'T WAIT

Watch this FREE WEBINAR now,
and Say "YES" to becoming a bestseller:

https://self-publishingschool.com/

Click on "Join Our Free Training"

About the Author

Luis is a Puerto Rican native and has built his career in the United States since 2001. He enjoys life with his wife Sara, and his sons, Caleb and Eli. He has a passion for developing careers and showing people how to be a better version of themselves. He has worked for almost 20 years with the youth, young adults and parents as a Director or counselor of multiple youth groups in various states in the Nation. Professionally he helps people of all ages find their full potential and reach their dreams.

How Can You Help?

Thank You for Reading My Book!

I really appreciate all of
your feedback, and I love
hearing what you have to say.

I need your input to make the
next version of this book and
my future books better.

Please leave me an honest review
on Amazon letting me know what
you thought of the book.

Thanks so much!

Luis A Andino

Made in the USA
Columbia, SC
05 September 2019